D1717114

Witness
the *Salem*

Witchcraft
Trials

with Elaine Landau

Titles in the
Explore Colonial America with Elaine Landau series

Celebrate the First Thanksgiving
with Elaine Landau
0-7660-2556-X

Celebrate the Founding of America
with Elaine Landau
0-7660-2557-8

Explore Colonial Jamestown
with Elaine Landau
0-7660-2554-3

Meet Ben Franklin
with Elaine Landau
0-7660-2555-1

Witness the Boston Tea Party
with Elaine Landau
0-7660-2553-5

Witness the Salem Witchcraft Trials
with Elaine Landau
0-7660-2558-6

Witness the *Salem Witchcraft Trials*

with Elaine Landau

Enslow Elementary

an imprint of

Enslow Publishers, Inc.

40 Industrial Road
Box 398
Berkeley Heights, NJ 07922
USA

http://www.enslow.com

For Emily and Allie

Enslow Elementary, an imprint of Enslow Publishers, Inc.

Enslow Elementary® is a registered trademark of Enslow Publishers, Inc.

Library of Congress Cataloging-in-Publication Data

Landau, Elaine.
    Witness the salem witchcraft trials with Elaine Landau / Elaine Landau.
        p. cm. — (Explore Colonial America with Elaine Landau)
    Includes bibliographical references and index.
    ISBN 0-7660-2558-6
    1. Trials (Witchcraft)—Massachusetts—Salem—Juvenile literature. 2. Witchcraft—Massachusetts—Salem—History—17th century—Juvenile literature. I. Title. II. Series.
    KFM2478.8.W5L36 2006
    133.4'3097445—dc22
                                                                            2005033801

Printed in the United States of America

10 9 8 7 6 5 4 3 2 1

To Our Readers: We have done our best to make sure all Internet Addresses in this book were active and appropriate when we went to press. However, the author and the publisher have no control over and assume no liability for the material available on those Internet sites or on other Web sites they may link to. Any comments or suggestions can be sent by e-mail to comments@enslow.com or to the address on the back cover.

Illustration Credits: 20th Century-Fox/Photofest, pp. 26, 40 (bottom); Associated Press, AP, pp. 38, 39 (top), 41; Bridgeman Art Library, p. 15; Clipart.com, pp. 10, 12, 37, 43 (top); Courtesy of the Salem Witch Museum, Salem, MA, pp. 8, 40 (top); David Pavelonis, Elaine and Max illustrations on pp. 1, 3, 5, 6, 7, 8, 9, 13, 15, 17, 21, 25, 29, 33, 37, 38, 41, 42; Elaine Landau, p. 42; Enslow Publishers, Inc., p. 6 (maps); Getty Images, p. 35; Hemera Technologies, Inc./Enslow Publishers, Inc./Library of Congress, backgrounds on pp. 5–9, 42–48; The Library of Congress, pp. 6 (right inset), 9, 17, 20, 28, 30, 34, p. 44 (top); © North Wind/North Wind Picture Archives, pp. 3, 4, 11, 14, 16, 18, 23, 29, 32, 33, 36, 39 (bottom two photos), 43 (bottom), 44 (bottom); Photograph courtesy Peabody Essex Museum, "Accusation of a Witch" by Elias C. Larrabee, Jr., p. 22; Photograph courtesy Peabody Essex Museum, "Examination of a Witch" by T. H. Matteson, p. 19.

Front Cover Illustrations: David Pavelonis (Elaine & Max); Hemera Technologies, Inc./Enslow Publishers, Inc./Library of Congress (collage at top); Photograph courtesy Peabody Essex Museum, "The Trial of George Jacobs" by T. H. Matteson (Trial image).

Back Cover Illustrations: David Pavelonis (Elaine & Max); Hemera Technologies, Inc./Enslow Publishers, Inc./Library of Congress (collage at top); © North Wind/North Wind Picture Archives (accused witch being arrested).

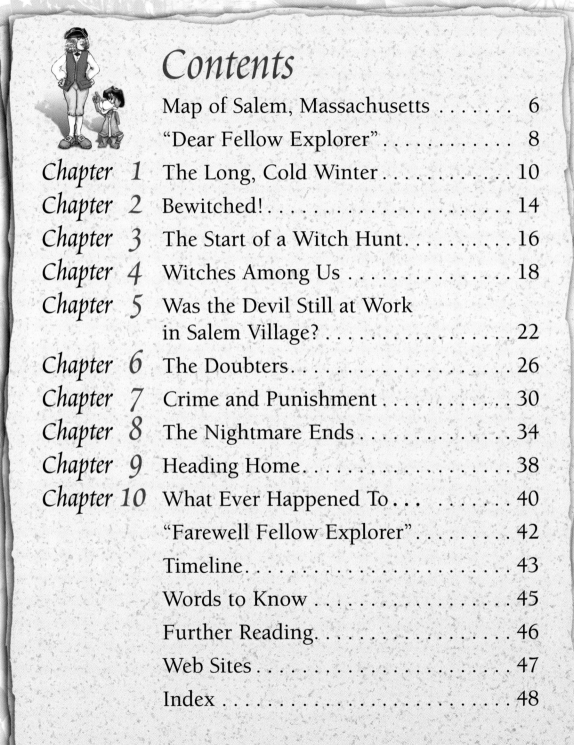

Contents

SALEM VILLAGE MASSACHUSETTS 1692

KEY

- ▭ = Bounds of village
- ▬ = Roads of village
- ■ = House of villager
- **X** = Place of execution

Wilkins Pond

Salem

NORTH AMERICA

Atlantic Ocean

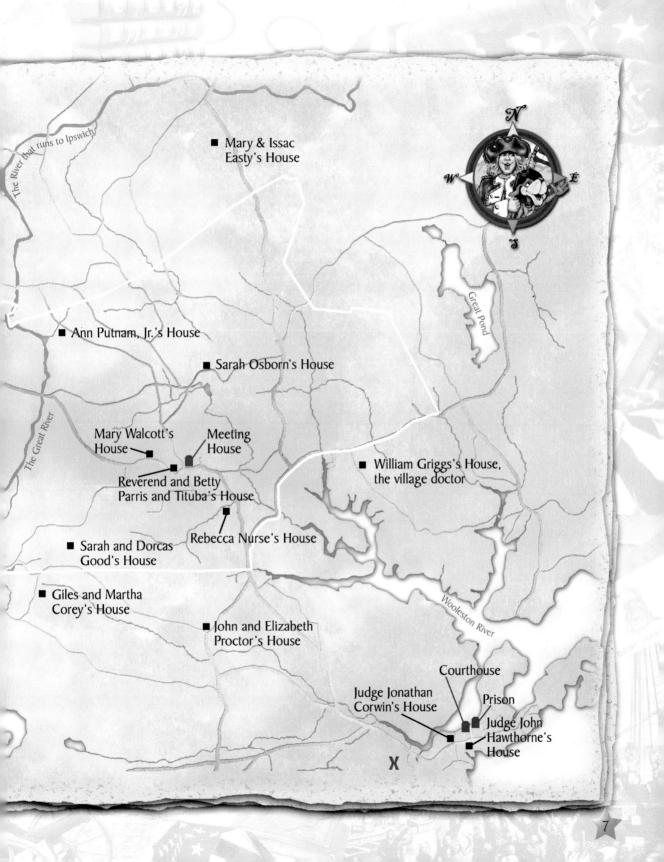

Mary & Issac
Easty's House

The River that runs to Ipswich

Great Pond

Ann Putnam, Jr.'s House

Sarah Osborn's House

The Great River

Mary Walcott's
House

Meeting
House

William Griggs's House,
the village doctor

Reverend and Betty
Parris and Tituba's House

Sarah and Dorcas
Good's House

Rebecca Nurse's House

Giles and Martha
Corey's House

Wooleston River

John and Elizabeth
Proctor's House

Courthouse

Judge Jonathan
Corwin's House

Prison

Judge John
Hawthorne's
House

X

Dear Fellow Explorer,

What if you could travel back in time? What would you want to see? You have heard about famous courtroom trials. Would you want to be at one?

Years ago, people thought that witches were real. They believed that they worked with the devil. People were taken to court for **witchcraft**. In 1692, it happened in the area we know today as Massachusetts.

Outside of the Salem Witch Museum is a statue of Roger Conant, the founder of Salem Village.

SALEM WITCH MUSEUM

In Salem, this house is often called "the witch house." It was once owned by Jonathan Corwin, one of the judges during the witch trials.

These trials became known as the Salem witchcraft trials.

I'm Elaine Landau and this is my dog, Max. Max and I do a lot of time traveling. Today we are going back to Salem Village.

Why not come along? Use this book as your time machine. Start your journey now—just turn the page.

The Long, Cold Winter

The trouble started during the bitter cold winter of 1691. **Blizzards** had struck the area for weeks. The heavy snows and freezing winds made it hard to be outdoors.

The young people of Salem Village were stuck inside. This was especially true for the girls. Unlike the boys, they did not even leave the home to hunt for animals. There was little for them to do. Often they felt lonely and bored.

Salem Village could be a lonely place in any case. It was miles from the town of Salem, which was a trade center. Salem Village was mostly made up of farms. There was a meetinghouse for religious services and not much else. Even these buildings were cold and uncomfortable during the winter. There never seemed to be enough firewood.

Salem's first meeting house was used for religious services.

Things were a bit better at the home of the village minister, Samuel Parris. His nine-year-old daughter, Betty, had her eleven-year-old cousin, Abigail, for company. Abigail Williams was an orphan who lived with the Parris family. She earned her keep by helping with household chores.

The girls also had Tituba. Tituba was one of the reverend's slaves. She had come from the island of Barbados in the Caribbean Sea, south of the United States we know today. Samuel Parris and his family had lived there for a time before coming to Salem Village. When he left the island, he brought a few slaves back with him. Tituba

In this drawing, Tituba tells tales to the children of Salem. The drawing is unfair because the artist made Tituba look like a witch.

told the girls stories about magic spells and powerful spirits. People often did such things in Barbados, but not in Salem Village.

Sometimes, young women from the village visited Betty and Abigail. Among these were twelve-year-old Ann Putnam and seventeen-year-old Elizabeth Hubbard. At times, nineteen-year-old Mercy Lewis and sixteen-year-old Mary Wolcott came. There were others too.

Many people believe that the young women begged Tituba to teach them fortune-telling games. Tituba may have told the girls to drop an egg white into a glass of water. The egg white would form a shape in a glass. The shape was supposed to be a sign of things to come.

This had to be done in secret. The people of Salem Village were Puritans. They believed in living strictly by the Bible. The Puritans felt that a person's life should be filled with hard work and prayer. Anything else invited the devil into their lives.

Reverend Parris insisted on strict religious teaching for Betty

One of the punishments for people accused of being witches was burning at the stake.

and Abigail. He led them in prayer every day. On Sundays, they spent hours in church listening to his sermons and singing hymns.

The Puritans wanted nothing to do with what they thought were spells or witchcraft. Witchcraft was both a sin and a crime in Salem Village. In some cases, it was punishable by death.

This fear of witchcraft was not new to the Puritans. The Puritans came from Europe where witchcraft trials were common in both Germany and England. Between 1560 and 1760, nearly one hundred thousand people were found guilty of witchcraft there.

In New England, the Puritans wanted to be rid of witches as well. As early as 1648, a woman in the Massachusetts Colony had been hanged for witchcraft.

Asking Tituba to speak of magic spells and fortune-telling was dangerous. Yet somehow that did not seem to matter to the girls that winter. After all, these were just some silly young people at play. Surely, no real harm could come from this—or could it?

② Bewitched!

In January 1692, Betty Parris began feeling ill. She was not hungry. Some days she would be forgetful or burst out crying. There were also times when Betty felt as though she was on fire.

At about the same time, Betty's cousin Abigail changed too. She would fall to the floor and shake. Sometimes

The girls of Salem would sometimes fall to the floor and shake. People thought witches had cast spells on them.

Reverend Samuel Parris was concerned when his daughter fell ill and started acting strangely.

she would just **babble**. It was as if she were speaking in a strange language.

The village doctor, William Griggs, was called. He examined the girls and found nothing physically wrong with either of them. At the time, people did not know about **mental illness**, or problems people have with the way they think and behave. Therefore, Griggs felt that they must have been bewitched.

The girls did not get any better. Instead, the unusual behavior spread. By mid-February, their friends began acting the same way. Now Ann Putnam, Elizabeth Hubbard, Mercy Lewis, Mary Wolcott, and others were thought to be **bewitched** too.

The villagers were upset. They wanted to know who had done this. Who was the witch among them?

3 The Start of a Witch Hunt

At first, the girls refused to point out the witch. This upset Reverend Parris. He did not want Satan, or the devil, in Salem Village. He especially did not want him near his own household.

Reverend Parris urged the girls to give names. Finally Betty said that Tituba had bewitched them. The girls also named two other women in Salem Village. These were Sarah Osborne and Sarah Good. They were women who the girls knew were not well liked by the villagers.

The three women named were likely choices. They were not very powerful. No one was going to come to their defense.

Sarah Osborne was an elderly woman. Her many health problems often kept her at home. She had not set foot in church for over a year. This was a sin among the Puritans.

The accused witches were hunted down and arrested.

The villagers used all types of devices to get the accused witches to talk. These people are in the stocks, which held their hands and necks and forced them to stand bent over. They were forced to do this for hours. Sometimes people threw things at them, like eggs and rotten fruit.

Few people liked Sarah Good. She was a poor homeless woman. Sarah Good often begged for food. Sometimes people gave her nothing. Then she would walk angrily away. She muttered things no one understood. Perhaps they thought that she had put a curse on them.

Tituba was a slave woman with no rights. She was at the mercy of Reverend Parris, who often beat her. At times, Tituba would say anything to avoid a whipping.

These women had not done spells together. They may not have even known one another. However, that did not change things. On February 29, 1692, all three women were arrested.

THE WITCHCRAFT TRIALS MADE PEOPLE THINK ABOUT THEIR OWN LIVES. IF A FENCE BLEW DOWN IN A STORM BEFORE, THEY THOUGHT IT WAS JUST BAD LUCK.

NOW THEY WERE SURE IT WAS WITCHCRAFT.

Witches Among Us

O n March 1, the three women were questioned at the village meetinghouse. The room was packed with people. Everyone was anxious to see those accused. They came to see the bewitched young women too. Weeks had passed and the young women had not gotten any better. Reverend Parris prayed for them every day. He asked the members of his church to pray for

A Puritan woman sits in a jail cell. This is the type of cell that would have held the accused witches.

Accused witches were often examined by doctors. People thought if a person had certain markings on his or her body then he or she was a witch.

them as well. When the young women did not improve, Parris ask other reverends from other towns to come to his home to pray. Yet, nothing helped those who seemed to be bewitched.

Two businessmen, Jonathan Corwin and John Hathorne, questioned the accused women. Neither had any legal training but this was not unusual. Law in Salem Village was based on the Bible. These men had studied that book well. Many respected men in the community would be appointed **magistrates** or judges when the actual trials began.

This painting shows the power that many Puritans thought that witches had at their command.

Both Sarah Osborne and Sarah Good claimed to be innocent. The bewitched young women showed that they felt differently. They would grunt, groan, and scream out during the questioning.

Only the slave woman Tituba confessed to being a witch. She may have thought that Reverend Parris would beat her if she did not. Or perhaps she thought the judges would be easier on her if she confessed.

In any case, Tituba described a tall man dressed in black. Sometimes he had a yellow bird with him. He was

supposed to be the devil. Tituba said that the man in black made her sign a book. She added that she had not been the only one from Salem Village to sign. Tituba said that four other women had signed and that Sarah Good and Sarah Osborne were among them. This was their **pact** or agreement with the devil.

Tituba told how the devil made her hurt the bewitched young women. She said that the devil would come to her in different forms. Sometimes, he looked like a hog, while other times he appeared as a large dog. Tituba said that she felt forced to do whatever he asked. She also spoke of frightening creatures such as huge red ants and talking cats.

The people believed Tituba. They thought that witches were real and feared their powers. They did not want to see evil at work in Salem Village.

After being questioned, the three accused women were taken to a jail in Boston. They would remain there until their actual trials.

But that did not end the trouble in Salem Village. It was just the start of things to come.

5

Was the Devil Still at Work in Salem Village?

Despite the arrests, the bewitched young women did not improve. The people of Salem Village prayed for help. They thought that God might be punishing their village. They wondered if the devil was still at work? Were there more witches among them?

The bewitched young women said there were. On March 11, Ann Putnam accused Martha Corey of

Soon enough, people were being accused of witchcraft all over Salem.

Martha Corey pleads for mercy during her trial.

witchcraft. Corey was not like the other accused women. She was a churchgoer.

However, Martha Corey was known to speak her mind. This was unusual in a Puritan woman. Some in Salem Village felt that Corey did not know how women were supposed to behave.

Martha Corey was questioned at the meetinghouse on March 21. She swore that she was innocent. Yet the bewitched young women made that hard to believe.

They twisted their bodies as if they were in terrible pain. The girls also copied every movement Corey made. If she shifted her feet, they shifted their feet. If Corey bit her lip, the girls would bite their lip. Then they would cry out in pain from the bite. Not surprisingly, Martha Corey was jailed.

Everyone was shocked when the next person was accused. It was seventy-one-year-old Rebecca Nurse. Rebecca Nurse never missed church. She was also known for her goodness.

Nevertheless, the bewitched young women insisted that she was a witch. Like Martha Corey, Rebecca Nurse was questioned. However, this time some of the village people spoke up for her. They reminded the magistrates of Nurse's kindness to others. It did not help. Nurse was soon jailed with the others.

By the end of March, five people had been locked up for witchcraft. Yet the witch-hunt had only just begun. The bewitched young women accused still more people.

Among these was Sarah Good's five-year-old daughter, Dorcas. After she confessed to being a witch, Dorcas went to jail as well. No one knows why Dorcas confessed. She may have been scared. It is also likely that the small child just wanted to be with her jailed mother. In April, Dorcas's mother, Sarah Good, gave birth to a baby while in jail. The baby stayed in prison with its mother and sister where it died a few weeks later.

Being jailed was not easy for young Dorcas. Despite her age, she was treated as harshly as an adult. However, the jailer's iron chains slipped off her tiny hands. Tiny iron handcuffs had to be made for her. The girl's family had to pay for these.

Rebecca Nurse's sister Mary Easty was also arrested. Like her sister, Easty attended church regularly. Before this, she had never been accused of any wrongdoing. Now she was questioned and sent to jail. Like the others, she would await trial there.

Women continued to be accused and jailed. Often, these were relatives of those already accused of witchcraft. Others had been in some sort of problem with one of the bewitched young women's families. Still others had openly doubted the bewitched young women's claims. Life was now very dangerous for many in Salem Village.

6 The Doubters

Not everyone in Salem Village believed the bewitched young women. Some people thought that they were "out of their wits" or **insane**. Others felt that they just wanted attention. Yet, few dared to question the young women. They feared that they might be accused of witchcraft as well.

That was what happened to a sixty-year-old tavern owner named John Proctor. Proctor did not believe the young

The Crucible was a movie about the Salem witch trials. Below, Judge Thomas Danforth, played by Paul Scofield, talks to Mary Warren, played by Karron Graves.

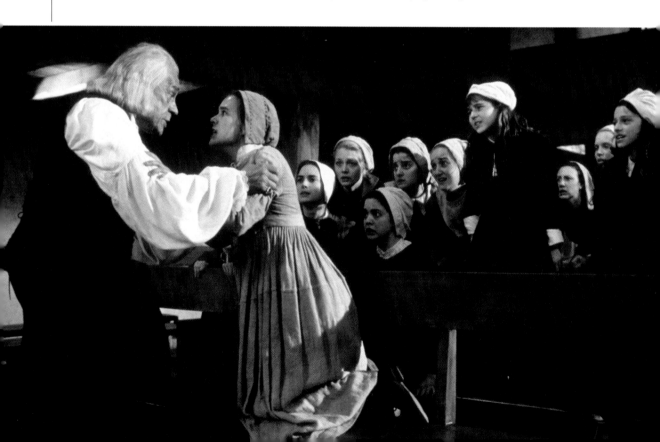

women were bewitched. He had even suggested that they "be had to the Whipping post." Proctor felt that the girls should be beaten rather than believed.

Then his young servant girl, Mary Warren, started acting bewitched. After Proctor threatened to beat her if she did not stop, Mary calmed down. However, before long, the troublesome behavior began again. Now Mary accused John Proctor's wife of being a witch. She said that Elizabeth Proctor tried to make her sign the devil's book.

> "We are all innocent persons."
>
> —John Proctor

That started a sad chain of events. On March 28, the bewitched young women accused Elizabeth Proctor of witchcraft too. They claimed that her spirit was choking them.

John Proctor went to his wife's hearing on April 11. He tried to defend her. Proctor insisted that his wife was innocent.

This angered her accusers. During the hearing, the girls claimed that John Proctor was a **wizard** (a male witch) as well. The Proctors were taken to jail.

Even ministers were being accused of witchcraft, like the Reverend George Burroughs. Though Burroughs used to be Salem Village's minister, he was now living in Maine.

Nevertheless, Ann Putnam accused him of being a wizard. On May 4, George Burroughs was arrested and brought to Salem Village for questioning. Burroughs made things worse for himself by publicly saying he did not believe in witches. The judges did not like their beliefs questioned. The bewitched girls did not like being doubted either.

Burroughs doubted that he would be treated fairly in Salem Village. He knew that the judges did not like him. He had quarreled with some of them before leaving for Maine. Burroughs was right. He was soon jailed.

As more people were accused, some began to question the idea of **spectral evidence**. This was the fact that a person could say in court that another person's spirit left his or her body and harmed others. No one could see these spirits except the bewitched young women.

That made it impossible for

This drawing of George Burroughs in chains appeared in Frank Leslie's illustrated newspaper in 1871.

the **accused**, those people who were on trial, to defend themselves. Those accused could not prove that an **invisible** (unseen) spirit had not left their bodies.

The judges accepted spectral evidence, but not everyone in Salem Village was comfortable with this. This was especially true when respected members of the community were accused. Yet before long, many people would be found guilty on spectral evidence alone.

As more people in Salem Village were accused, some began to doubt whether there were any witches at all.

Crime and Punishment

The trials of the accused began in mid-June. By then, over 150 of the 1,680 people living in Salem Village had been jailed for witchcraft. The nine trial judges were appointed by William Phips, the Massachusetts Colony's governor.

The court's chief justice was William Stoughton. He was a deeply religious man who believed in spectral evidence. Jonathan Corwin and John Hathorne were among the other judges as well.

Some of the accused never even made it to trial. Sarah Osborne died in jail before being tried. So did three others.

When the trials began, the juries heard the evidence against the accused. They watched while the bewitched girls twitched, screamed, and pointed to those on trial. The judges did not even try to quiet them.

Sarah Good was found guilty and sentenced to hang. While in jail, she tried to kill herself three

William Stoughton was the chief judge during the trials.

times. Then on July 19, she was taken outside and hanged.

Before she was hanged, a minister named Nicholas Noyes spoke to Sarah Good. He told her to confess to save her soul. Good answered: "You're a liar! I am no more a witch than you are a wizard! If you take away my life, God will give you blood to drink."

On the day Sarah Good was put to death, Rebecca Nurse and three others were hanged as well, and the executions continued.

On August 19, five more people were hanged. These included John Proctor and George Burroughs. Following the hangings, the bodies were dumped into a common grave. George Burroughs had worn his best suit. Thieves took the suit from his lifeless body after he was buried.

Just before dying, Burroughs said the Lord's Prayer perfectly. Since Puritans believed that a witch or wizard could not do this, Burrough's prayer made the crowd uneasy. They thought he might have been innocent. However, he was hanged anyway.

The hangings did not stop. Eight more people were **executed** on September 22. Among these were Mary Easty and Martha Corey.

Giles Corey, Martha Corey's husband, had been accused as well. When asked if he was a wizard, seventy-year-old Giles Corey refused to answer. He knew no

Reverend George Burroughs stunned the crowds in Salem by saying the Lord's Prayer perfectly before he was hanged.

Giles Corey (on the left) was accused by a witness as well.

one would believe he was innocent.

Corey was **tortured** to make him confess. Heavy stones were placed on his body, which killed him two days later. Despite the pain, Giles Corey did not confess.

Others were less brave. Many admitted to crimes they did not do. Those who confessed and **repented**, or said they were sorry, lived. The people who insisted they were innocent hanged. That was how things were in Salem Village.

THE COURT HOPED TO MAKE GILES COREY CONFESS.

GILES COREY BECAME A HERO INSTEAD. SONGS WERE EVEN WRITTEN ABOUT HIS BRAVERY.

8 The Nightmare Ends

Sometimes it seemed as if the Salem Village witchcraft trials would never end. Yet they did. The last eight people were executed on September 22. In all, twenty people had been killed. Nineteen were hanged, and Giles Corey died while being tortured.

By that time, many people were tired of all the arrests and hangings. The bewitched young women had even accused some relatives of the judges. No one was going to put those people on trial.

On September 29, Massachusetts Governor Phips returned from a trip to Maine. He had wanted the trials and punishments finished before his return. Instead, he found over one hundred people still in jail awaiting trial.

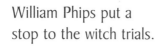

William Phips put a stop to the witch trials.

The trials had hurt Salem Village. They had taken up too much of the villagers' time and energy. Farms and business suffered. The jailings and executions left young children without parents. Bad feelings had deepened between the families and friends of the accused and their accusers.

Governor Phips knew that things had gone too far.

He had to take action. So on October 8, he ordered that there be no further arrests or trials for witchcraft. Then on October 29, he closed the court set up to hear these cases. The nightmare was finally over.

Hundreds of years later, some still wonder how those unfair trials could have happened. People have written books and plays about it. One play, *The Crucible*, was written by Arthur Miller in 1953. Loosely based on the events in Salem Village, it shows the dangers of witch hunts.

Playwright Arthur Miller (right) bows after a performance of *The Crucible*.

There are no clear answers to explain what happened in Salem Village. The trouble may have started because some bored young women wanted attention. After that, much of Salem Village may have simply become caught up in the frenzy of a witch hunt. Or was there more to it?

Many of the accused were disliked by the Putnam family. Rebecca Nurse may have been among these. She had been involved in a dispute with them some time ago. The Putnams were a large and powerful Salem Village family. Young Ann Putnam accused quite a number of people. After a while, Ann's mother also appeared bewitched. She began accusing people of witchcraft as well. However, Ann's mother had a long history of mental problems.

Some historians feel that land may have had a lot to do with the trials. People found guilty of witchcraft lost all their property. Some of the accused owned plots of land that many villagers wanted. The other villagers were eager to buy these plots cheaply.

Other reasons have been given to explain what happened in Salem Village as well. **Psychologist** (someone who studies the mind) Linnda Caporael thinks that the bewitched girls might have had ergot poisoning. Ergot is a fungus that grows on grains. At the time of the witchcraft trials, rye was grown in the area and people in Salem Village ate rye bread. Ergot poisoning could have caused much of the behavior the girls displayed.

After the trials, Judge Sewell withdrew the guilty verdicts.

Still another reason for the witchcraft trials may be tied to the settlers' fears about the local Indians. During the 1670s and 1680s, fighting with the Wabanaki Indians took its toll on the settlers. Many on New England's frontier lost family members, homes, and livestock (farm animals) during attacks. Some who survived settled in Salem Village and the surrounding area.

Ergot can be seen as the thick pieces on this stalk of rye.

The Puritans believed that the Indian attacks, like witchcraft, were caused by the devil. They were anxious to see an end to both. Therefore, it may not be surprising that the witchcraft trials took place.

People often blame the bewitched young women for what happened. Yet the Salem Village adults are also to blame for taking them seriously. They arrested, tried, and hanged the accused.

Many important individuals in the area also did not do enough to stop it. They only spoke out once their family members were accused. Without a doubt, the blame for what happened in Salem Village must be shared.

AFTER THE TRIALS, SOME JURY MEMBERS APOLOGIZED. THEY KNEW THAT THEY HAD FOUND INNOCENT PEOPLE GUILTY.

THE FAMILIES OF SOME OF THE VICTIMS RECEIVED MONEY FOR THEIR LOSSES AS WELL.

Heading Home

9

Y ou cannot find Salem Village on a map today. In 1752, it became the town of Danvers, Massachusetts.

Danvers has many witchcraft museums. You can still visit Jonathan Corwin's house or Rebecca Nurse's farm. A monument and small park in Danvers honors those who died because of the trials.

Well, we learned a lot about the colonists of Salem Village. It seems the villagers learned an important lesson, too. "Justice" must always be fair and truly just. The Salem witchcraft trials are an important reminder of that.

Max and I are glad you came to Salem Village with us. Time travel is always more fun with friends. To the time machine!

A Salem, Massachusetts, police officer sits in his car, which shows a witch as part of the town symbol.

THIS MEMORIAL LISTS ALL THE NAMES OF THE VICTIMS OF THE WITCHCRAFT TRIALS.

IT'S FITTING THAT THEY ARE REMEMBERED.

This wall in Salem is a memorial to those people who were executed during the witch trials. Each stone bench sticking out from the wall has a person's name carved into it.

MARTHA COREY
HANGED
SEPT. 22, 1692

GILES COREY
PRESSED TO DEATH
SEPT. 19. 1692

10 What Ever Happened To . . .

Max and I meet lots of people when time traveling. Sometimes we wonder what became of them. Here are a few answers:

Ann Putnam

In 1706, Ann Putnam publicly said she was sorry for her role in the Salem witchcraft trials. She never married, and she died when she was just thirty-seven years old.

Dorcas Good

As a five year old, Dorcas remained jailed for nearly eight months. After her release, she was no longer the healthy cheerful child she had been. She became quiet and sad and seemed to lose interest in life. Some say that she later went insane.

The Salem Witch Museum at nighttime

Tituba

Charlyne Woodard played Tituba in the 1996 movie *The Crucible*, which was about the Salem witch trials.

Tituba remained in jail nearly a year longer than the others arrested for witchcraft. Prisoners had to pay for their room and board while jailed. Reverend Parris would not pay Tituba's bill. Finally, someone bought Tituba from Parris and paid her debt. Though out of jail, she remained a slave.

Reverend Samuel Parris

Following the witchcraft trials, support for Reverend Parris lessened. He had not remained open-minded about those accused. Instead, Parris had given several sermons in which he preached against them. Rebecca Nurse's relatives were especially against him remaining reverend of the church. In 1697, Parris left Salem Village to become a minister in western Massachusetts. In time, he left there too. After that, he worked as a schoolteacher and merchant.

This statue in the Salem Wax Museum of Witches and Seafarers serves as a memorial to those who lost their lives during the trials.

WHAT EVER HAPPENED TO BETTY PARRIS?

REVEREND PARRIS SENT HER TO LIVE WITH A CLOSE FAMILY FRIEND. OUT OF SALEM, SHE NO LONGER FELT BEWITCHED. SHE LATER MARRIED AND HAD FIVE CHILDREN.

Farewell Fellow Explorer,

I just wanted to tell you about the real "Max and me." I am a children's book author and Max is a small, fluffy, white dog. I almost named him Marshmallow because of how he looks. However, he seems to think he's human—so only a more dignified name would do!

Max also seems to think that he is a large, powerful dog. He fearlessly chases after much larger dogs in the neighborhood. Max was thrilled when the artist for this book drew him as a dog several times his size. He felt that someone in the art world had finally captured his true spirit.

In real life, Max is quite a traveler. I have taken him to nearly every state while doing research for different books. We live in Florida, so when we go north I have to pack a sweater for him. When we were in Oregon it rained, and I was glad I brought his raincoat.

None of this gear is necessary for time traveling. My "take off" spot is the computer station, and as always Max sits faithfully by my side.

Best Wishes,
Elaine & Max
(a small dog with big dreams)

Timeline

1691   Salem Village experiences a brutally cold winter.

1692   **January**—Betty Parris and Abigail Williams begin behaving strangely and are thought to be bewitched.

mid-February—A number of young women in Salem Village show signs of being bewitched.

February 29—Warrants for the arrest of Tituba, Sarah Good, and Sarah Osborne are issued.

March 1—Tituba, Sarah Good, and Sarah Osborne are questioned at the meetinghouse.

March 11—Martha Corey is accused of witchcraft.

March 21—Martha Corey is questioned at the meetinghouse.

March 28—Elizabeth Proctor is accused of witchcraft.

April 11—Elizabeth Proctor is questioned at the meetinghouse. John Proctor is accused of being a wizard.

May 4—George Burroughs is arrested for being a wizard and brought to Salem from Maine to be questioned.

mid-June—The actual trials begin.

Timeline

July 19—Sarah Good, Rebecca Nurse, and others are executed for witchcraft.

August 19—Five more people are hanged, including John Proctor and George Burroughs.

September 19—Giles Corey is tortured to death. Heavy stones were placed on his body.

September 22—Eight people are hanged, including Martha Corey and Mary Easty.

September 29—Governor Phips returns from a trip to Maine.

October 8—Governor Phips orders that there will be no further arrests or trials for witchcraft.

October 29—The court set up to handle the witchcraft cases is dissolved.

1697 Reverend Samuel Parris leaves Salem Village.

1703 A law is passed in Massachusetts forbidding the use of spectral evidence in trials.

1706 Ann Putnam apologizes for her role in the Salem witchcraft trials.

1752 Salem Village becomes the town of Danvers, Massachusetts.

Words to Know

babble—To speak as if in a strange language.

bewitched—Having had a spell cast on one by a witch.

blizzard—A large snowstorm.

execute—To take someone's life as punishment for a crime.

insane—Having problems with the way one thinks or behaves.

magistrate—A judge.

pact—An agreement.

psychologist—Someone who studies the mind.

repent—To be sorry for wrongdoing.

spectral evidence—A statement in court that a person's spirit left his or her body and harmed others.

torture—To cause a person great physical pain.

witchcraft—Black or evil magic.

wizard—A male thought to have magic powers.

Further Reading

Asirvathan, Sandy. *The Salem Witch Trials*. Philadelphia, Chelsea House Publishers, 2002.

Boraas, Tracey. *The Salem Witch Trials*. Mankato, Minn.: Capstone Press, 2004.

Burgan, Michael. *The Salem Witch Trials*. Minneapolis, Minn.: Compass Point Books, 2005.

Dolan, Edward F. *The Salem Witch Trials*. Tarrytown, N.Y.: Benchmark Books, 2002.

Martin, Michael. *Salem Witch Trials*. Mankato, Minn.: Capstone Press, 2005.

Yolen, Jane and Stemple Heidi. *The Salem Witch Trials: An Unsolved Mystery From History*. New York: Simon & Schuster, 2004.

Web Sites

National Geographic: Salem Witch-Hunt-Interactive

Experience what it was like to be accused of witchcraft during the 1692 Salem witchcraft trials in this exciting online trial.

    <http://www.nationalgeographic.com/salem/>

Salem Wax Museum of Witches and Seafarers

Experience the terror of the Salem Witch Trials of 1692, but do not miss the link marked "Education" on this fascinating Web site.

    <http://www.salemwaxmuseum.com>

Salem Witch Museum

Visit this Web site to see what it was like to be a Salem Villager in 1692. This Web site has some wonderful pictures.

    <http://www.salemwitchmuseum.com>

Index